Topz

10

THINGS EVERY GIRL NEEDS TO KNOW

TOPZ 10 THINGS EVERY GIRL NEEDS TO KNOW ...

Welcome to this snazzy and ever-so-handy **TOPZ 10** guide to living life the way God means you to. We, the Topz Gang, want to help you live the totally best way – with God right by your side!

Have you ever been on a car journey with someone who has a sat nav? (Did you know that's short for 'Satellite Navigation' device? Ugh! Too many long words!) Anyway, a sat nav is *really* useful when you're off somewhere in the car and you don't know the way. You just pop in the postcode for where you want to go and, as you're driving along – well, not YOU obviously but whoever's the driver – it says helpful things like, 'Turn left', or 'Turn right', or if you've gone in the wrong direction, 'Turn around'.

Sat navs guide you. They explain to you what to do while you're doing it and if you follow the instructions a sat nav gives you and stick to the right roads – in the end, you should wind up in the right place.

So we all had a think: if a car sat nav helps to guide our car journeys, wouldn't it be just the most fandabulously brilliant thing in the world to have a 'life sat nav' to help guide our *life* journeys!

And then *that* got us thinking even more about what we think are the **TOPZ 10** things every girl should know to get the most out of their lives! Get these **TOPZ 10** things straight and you will be set on the right road, going in the right direction!

So, just like a sat nav, this book will guide you every day. It will help you to get close to God so that He can show you how to grow into the person He always intended you to be. He'll lead you through even the trickiest stuff. With God, you never need to feel lost or on your own.

Sound good? Then get set! Trace over the letters on the next page and when you've finished, shout the words out loud!

I'm ready!

1

GOD MADE YOU

'In the beginning' (Genesis 1 v 1) are the very first words in the Bible – which makes perfect sense really, being at the beginning of God's Book! And when the Bible says 'the beginning', it means the very, very, *very* beginning! Before God had even created light or the sky, let alone Planet Earth with everything that was needed so that people like us could live there – could *survive* there!

But after God had done all that, after He'd created an entire universe and the earth within it, full of living, growing plants and animals and fish – that's when He thought, 'Actually, what I *really want* now is some friends.'

So *that's* when God created the very first human beings – a man called Adam and a woman called Eve. He gave them a beautiful garden to live in and look after. He talked with them; He spent time with them. **GOD HAD CREATED THEM AND GOD LOVED THEM.**

What's your first (your Christian) name? Write it in the space below, then decorate it with swirls and squiggles and the most fantastical patterns your brain can come up with. Use as many different colours as you can. See how super-funky you can make it!

So – do you like what you've done? Have you made your name look super-amazing? Totally fab and like *the* best name in the whole world?

Because the thing is, the God who is powerful and creative enough to have made the universe; the God who is brilliant and loving and generous enough to have decided to make people to live in it – that same powerful, creative, brilliant, loving, FANTASTIC God – made you. That's right – YOU!

And He didn't just have some vague idea in His mind when He put you together either. He knew exactly what He wanted.

'God has made us what we are' (Ephesians 2 v 10).

Isn't that exciting! God made you and me and all of us exactly the way we are. And He loves everything about us. He created each of us to be different and to have a special friendship with Him.

In other words, you're here because God *wants* you to be here. You're here because God has a purpose for you and for your life. So stick close to Him! He cares about you and knows what's best for you.

Have another look at your name on the previous page. What do you think of the way you've made it look now? Does it need any more colours? Can you give it a bit more glitz? A bit more *va-va-voom*? **BECAUSE YOU ARE A ONE-OFF.** A unique creation. Loved by God and made by Him – *exactly* the way He intended you to be.

Life with God is definitely an adventure. Oh yes, it is!

The Bible is full of stories about women and men whose lives have turned into the most extraordinary adventures because they decided to say YES to God. They might have been scared, and they might have worried that they weren't good enough or brave enough or clever enough to be used by God. But in the end, they still made up their minds to obey Him and to trust Him.

TO LET GOD TAKE THEIR LIVES AND TURN THEM INTO ADVENTURERS FOR HIM!

The New Testament tells the story of perhaps one of the bravest woman adventurers to have ever lived.

Do you know who she is? Unjumble the letters below and write her name in the space. (Easy-peasy, right?)

RMYA

You got it – **Mary**. A very wonderful Mary.

Mary, who became the mother of God's very own Son, Jesus – because that's what God chose her to be.

Faced with something so huge and so frightening – after all, an angel was in her house telling her that God *Himself* wanted her to carry His baby! – did Mary shake her head and say, 'No, thanks'? Or, 'Not sure I can be bothered'? Or, 'Me? You must be joking'?

No! Mary listened to the angel. She heard what God wanted her to do. She said, 'I am the Lord's servant ... may it happen to me as you have said' (Luke 1 v 38).

And by saying, 'Yes, God', Mary brought Jesus, God's Son, into the world. Jesus: who was born on earth to make it possible for everyone everywhere – that includes you! – to be God's friends forever.

I think that deserves a bit of a something, don't you? Trace over the letters, then shout the word out as loudly as you dare!

WOW!

So, Mary said YES to God. She started out on the greatest adventure of her life because God had a purpose for her.

You see, people had turned away from God through the bad things they'd said and the wrong things they'd done. They'd been selfish and unkind. They'd ignored Him and disobeyed Him, even though He'd looked after them and loved them. And because of that, God knew He had to punish them.

But *He decided not to* because of how much He loved them.

HUH?

God came up with a plan: instead of the people He'd created being punished, He would send His Son, Jesus, to take that punishment instead. And now, when any of us believe that Jesus is God's Son, and are sorry for the wrong things we've done, we are saved to live with God forever.

Starting right here, right now!

Stonking!

Which brings us right back to Mary. God's purpose for Mary was to be the mother of His Son, Jesus. And because Mary chose to obey Him and say, 'Yes, God', she became a vital part in His plan to save the world. What an amazing adventure for her! And what a mega-incredible lady!

Imagine the angel arriving in Mary's house and telling her what God wanted her to do. Write down here how you think Mary might have felt:

_____

_____

What about you? If you knew God wanted you to do something special for Him – even if it seemed scary or difficult – would you say yes?

Just remember that God will always make you brave enough and strong enough for the adventures He has planned for you. Because, just like Mary, you're more than just precious to Him.

TO GOD, YOU ARE PRICELESS.

In the Topz Gang, we have loads of adventures.

We go on cycling trips and have leapfrog races.

We zoom really fast down at the park in my homemade go-kart.

We had a muffin-baking day for a cake stall to raise money for the homeless shelter in Holly Hill. So many muffins!

We won first prize in the garden show for a sunflower we planted and took it in turns to water – it was huge!

We put on a play at church that we'd written ourselves.

We helped my neighbour for a whole month when she was ill in bed, by doing all her shopping and housework.

We went camping with our youth club and woke up one morning to find our field full of sheep!

The best thing about adventures is that God wants to be right beside us through all of them. **_HE LOVES TO SHARE EVERY MOMENT OF EVERY DAY WITH US._**

What adventures have you had, with your friends or with your family?

Think of some of the best ones, and use the space on the next page to write them down. Then, if you ever have a day when you feel a bit bored or a bit gloomy, read over them to inspire you to plan some new adventures – with God by your side!

Cool! You're some adventurer, you know that?!

15

Now write down some adventures you'd *like* to have in the future – maybe places you'd like to go to, or things you'd like to see, or people or organisations you'd like to help ...

_____

_____

_____

_____

_____

_____

God made you! That's number 1 of our Topz 10!

If you believe or want to start believing that God made you, then pray this prayer ...

Thank You, Father God, that You made me exactly the way I am and have a purpose for me. Help me to remember that You are always right beside me as I go on the adventures You have planned for me. Amen.

GOD LOVES YOU

Have you ever had a really bad day? I mean *really* bad?
I had one last week. First I didn't put the lid on my water
bottle properly before I put it in my bag. By the time I got
to school, my books and my PE kit were soaked through.
Then I got in trouble because I forgot I was on classroom
tidy duty at morning break. At lunchtime, I tripped over
my shoelace and knocked into our head teacher who
just happened to be carrying a full cup of coffee, which
ended up all over him. Then, when I got home, I realised
I'd left my homework for the next day behind, so I
couldn't do it! See? **TOLD YOU IT WAS BAD!**

Stuff happens. It just does. Just as you can wake up to
sunshine and five minutes later it's raining, so a day can
start off brilliantly – but then things start to go wrong
and suddenly you don't feel so good about yourself.

By the end of *my* bad day I felt stupid and useless
and like the clumsiest, most forgetful person on the
planet! I wouldn't even let Josie come round in the
evening to cheer me up in case I did something else
mega tragic and she decided I was the worst friend ever
and didn't want to hang out with me anymore!

Feeling good about ourselves isn't always easy, is it?

Do you ever find yourself thinking you'll never be as clever as someone else in your class? Or as talented as that other girl? Or as popular?

Or maybe something has happened and you've felt like me after my bad day – afraid that your friends won't want to have anything to do with you anymore.

Sometimes it's our own thoughts that make us feel bad about ourselves. And that's hard enough.

But sometimes, too, it can be because of things other people say. Unkind things. Thoughtless things. Things that aren't even true. But they can *feel* true to us. They can really hurt us.

They can affect how we see ourselves and make us feel a bit worthless. A bit second, or even ninth or tenth best.

Well, let's sort out one thing right now! Does God think you're second, or ninth or tenth, best? Trace over the letters ...

That's right – NO!

So, what DOES God think of you?

Let's start with some lists. Who do you think the absolute world of? Maybe your mum or your dad or someone else who looks after you, a favourite teacher, a best friend, a cousin, a brother or a sister. Write down their name here:

_____

Now think about all the reasons why you like them or love them so much. Is it because they're kind or funny, patient or generous, clever or talented? Whatever it is about them that means so much to you, write it all down in a list here:

OK, so this next list might seem a bit trickier. Think of it as another challenge. I love a good challenge!

Now write another list of positive things, but this time, positive things about YOURSELF. Ask a friend to help you, or you could even ask the person you've written about on the previous page. Get them to tell you what they really like about you, then write it all down and believe it! After all, if someone else can see it – it's got to be true!

You sound like just my kind of friend!

And if you're wondering what any of this has to do with what God thinks of you, it's this:

When God looks at you, He sees all the good bits! He sees all the truly positive things that make up who you are.

Just as you can write a list of the things you really like about your best friend, or your cousin, or whoever it is you wrote about, so God can add to that list of brilliant things you've written about yourself. He can see even *more* of what makes you wonderful and special and a totally one-off amazing creation!

He can see it all – because He put you together in the first place. You see, however you feel about yourself some days, God's view of you never changes. **TO HIM YOU ARE PRECIOUS.** You will always matter.

Here are a few verses from the Bible that tell us how special we are to God:

'you belong to the Lord your God ... he chose you' (Deuteronomy 7 v 6).

'You created every part of me ... you saw me before I was born' (Psalm 139 v 13, 16).

'Even the hairs of your head have all been counted' (Luke 12 v 7).

'See how much the Father has loved us! His love is so great that we are called God's children' (1 John 3 v 1).

If someone gives me a choice, I always find it quite hard to make up my mind. Crisps: prawn cocktail or salt and vinegar? Sweets: mints or chocolate? Apple crumble: best with ice cream or custard? And then, if I finally *do* make up my mind, a second later I've changed it again!

It's true – Benny can be a nightmare!

Well, here's the good news. God isn't like Benny.

HE DOESN'T CHANGE HIS MIND.

God loves you today and He'll love you tomorrow, the next day and always. He *won't* change His mind. Whatever happens, you will always be His precious daughter.

'For I am certain that ... there is nothing in all creation that will ever be able to separate us from the love of God which is ours through Christ Jesus our Lord' (Romans 8 v 38–39).

So – what can change the way God feels about you? (Trace over the letters!)

NOTHING

One of the people written about in the Bible is a man called Zacchaeus. Have you heard of him? His story is pretty cool!

If you ever find yourself thinking that maybe you're not good enough for God to love – remember a little man called Zacchaeus.

Zacchaeus did LOTS of things wrong. He worked as a tax collector, which didn't make him very popular to start with. But the bad part was that he was a *dishonest* tax collector.

He cheated people out of their money. He stole from them. In fact, Zacchaeus was probably one of the most hated people in the town of Jericho when Jesus arrived there.

But of all the people Jesus could have gone to have a meal with – all the good and fair people, the honest and kind people – **IT WAS ZACCHAEUS HE CHOSE.**

Why? Because Zacchaeus was about as far away from God as anyone could be. He didn't live his life at all the way God wanted him to.

But God didn't turn His back on Zacchaeus. He didn't say, 'Sorry, Zac, after everything you've done, you'll never be good enough.'

No. God loved him all the same, and wanted Zacchaeus to be His friend.

So, Jesus called to him, went round to his house, and told Zacchaeus all about God's love for him. And right then and there, Zacchaeus said he was sorry for the wrong things he'd been doing and became God's newest friend. (You can read his story in the book of Luke in the New Testament of the Bible, chapter 19 and verses 1 to 10.)

You see? If you do find yourself having a bad day like mine at the start of this chapter and you end up feeling a bit rubbishy THEN STOP and remember:

- **God created every part of you and saw you before you were even born.**

- **God has counted every hair on your head.**

- **God has made you what you are.**

- **You belong to God – your Father in heaven.**

- **Oh yes, and don't forget God's new friend, Zacchaeus, either!**

So that's number 2 of our Topz 10: God loves you!

Why not say this prayer now …

Dear God, thank You for Your amazing love for me – love that is so big and wide and long and deep that there isn't a single chance it will ever run out! You loved me yesterday, You love me today and You will love me tomorrow – no matter what! You love me just as I am. And I don't need to work for Your love, I just need to accept it and love You in return. I love You, God, from the bottom of my heart. Amen.

3 GOD HAS GOOD PLANS FOR YOU

Do you like making plans? Sarah and me – **WE'RE ALWAYS PLANNING STUFF!** We like working out what we might do at the weekend. Sometimes it could be just meeting up at the park or the shopping centre. Or maybe going ice skating with the rest of the Topz Gang like we did last weekend. And we talk about way, way ahead in the future, too. Once, we decided that when we grow up, we should run an animal rescue centre together!

Making plans can be really exciting! People plan all sorts of things:

- **What they're going to do at the weekend.**
- **What they're going to be when they grow up.**
- **Where they're going to go on holiday.**
- **Where they might move house to.**
- **What books they're going to read next.**
- **What film they're going to see at the cinema.**

Right now, Dad's planning what new car he's going to buy!

Have you got any plans at the moment? Or are there any plans you'd like to make, either for right now or for some time in the future? Have a think and write them down here:

What you want to do – today, tomorrow, next week, next year – is important. The ideas you have, the decisions you make – your hopes and dreams – are all a part of YOU. They matter.

As you get older, you'll find you have more and more decisions to make, more and more 'future' stuff to plan: what will you be when you grow up? Where might you want to live? Who will be your best friend for life?

> **Josie, of course! No contest!**

Haha! Thanks, Sarah!

Because God knows us so well, He understands what we want and why we may want it. He knows the things we get excited about; the things we love to do.

He sees our 'big' dreams and He wants us to be happy.

And it's because God wants us to be happy that He hopes we'll come to Him to talk through our plans and ideas.

GOD LOVES US TO CHAT TO HIM ABOUT EVERYTHING. The closer we keep to Him through talking to Him regularly and reading what He has to teach us in the Bible, the more He can help us make wise choices and decisions when it comes to making plans.

And if we're properly tuned in to God, we should start to find that our 'big' plans fall in line with His 'big' plans for us.

Fancy a bit of a quiz? Here's a list of goals or dreams people might have. Read them through and think about which ones God would think are good, and which ones probably need a bit of a rethink. Then tick a box for each one.

Good   Rethink

When I grow up, I want lots of money so I can have everything I want. ☐ ☐

I want to live in a massive house one day – just me, no one else! ☐ ☐

I want to work hard and be really good at my job. ☐ ☐

All I want is to be famous. ☐ ☐

I want to find ways to help people who don't have as much as I do. ☐ ☐

When I'm older, I want to use my spare time to volunteer for a charity. ☐ ☐

When I'm earning money, I'm going to spend it all on clothes. ☐ ☐

When I have a job, I'm going to save some money regularly to give to the homeless shelter. ☐ ☐

How do you think God would feel about your answers?

To answer that question, ask yourself what you know about God. If you read your Bible and talk to God regularly, you probably know Him quite well. Even what you've read in this book so far will have given you a good idea of what your heavenly Father is like. And just you wait – you're going to find out a whole lot more!

God is full of love – but there are some things He hates, too:

He hates to see people hurting each other.

He hates selfishness and greed.

He hates lies and dishonesty.

He hates injustice.

God forgives people for the wrong things they do and for the wrong ways they think and behave – but He still hates those wrong things. **BECAUSE HE IS PERFECT.** Because He is holy.

Knowing all that about God – how truly loving He really is – does that change any of the boxes you've ticked on the previous page?

Now think about some of your own plans. Maybe for now; maybe for the future. How do they fit in with God's character?

This is a great way of testing your plans – to see if you're doing what God would want you to do. If you plan to do something that is very far from being 'God-like', then you can be fairly sure that God wouldn't think it's a good plan. **SO MAYBE IT NEEDS A RETHINK.**

But God isn't out to spoil our fun. No! He knows that what we want matters to us. He just wants to guide us so that the decisions and choices we make are the best for us. So in the end we'll have MORE fun because we'll be going His way, not our own way – which can sometimes be a little bit selfish!

You see, God doesn't just see what's happening here and now, the way we do. He sees something much bigger than that. He sees everything! Which is why the best possible thing we can do when we need to decide something important, or work on a plan, is to check it all out with God.

God has plans for you, after all! Good plans!

'I alone know the plans I have for you, plans to bring you prosperity and not disaster, plans to bring about the future you hope for' (Jeremiah 29 v 11).

There are some other Topz ways to check that your ideas are good with God, too:

Never forget God! **He's with you every day, just waiting to help you out.**

'Remember the LORD in everything you do, and he will show you the right way' (Proverbs 3 v 6).

Talk to God! **If you want to know what someone thinks about something, you ask them, don't you? It's the same with God – so ask Him!**

'It is the LORD who gives wisdom; from him come knowledge and understanding' (Proverbs 2 v 6).

Trust God **to show you what to do. Try not to think that you know better than He does.**

'Trust in the LORD with all your heart. Never rely on what you think you know' (Proverbs 3 v 5).

> *Don't get impatient! God might not show you the right thing straightaway. Sometimes you just have to wait – and keep on asking.*

'Look for [knowledge] as hard as you would for silver or some hidden treasure' (Proverbs 2 v 4).

> *Always remember God's rules for life. Ask yourself if what you want to do fits in with them.*

'simply obey the LORD and refuse to do wrong' (Proverbs 3 v 7).

> *Listen to your conscience! If you're planning to do something and a little voice inside you is saying, 'Hmm, not sure about that!' – don't ignore it. It could be God.*

'Avoid evil and walk straight ahead' (Proverbs 4 v 27).

> *Talk to other Christians. People who have known God for a long time. Tell them your plans – and listen to their advice.*

'Listen to what is wise and try to understand it' (Proverbs 2 v 2).

Woah! There's a lot to think about, isn't there?

So, time for some fun! Here's a list of words from this chapter about letting God guide you when you're making big plans. Can you find them all in the word search?

D	E	C	I	S	I	O	N	S	E	R	O	J	U
A	B	S	A	M	N	O	H	Q	E	U	R	H	U
B	T	D	I	E	P	A	S	M	K	L	W	C	D
S	B	R	T	W	P	A	E	T	S	E	B	H	E
G	E	S	U	P	C	M	T	G	U	S	T	A	T
T	I	C	Y	S	B	K	N	I	H	T	E	R	I
L	W	J	I	E	T	W	D	S	E	Y	X	A	C
X	F	K	R	O	C	T	N	B	H	N	W	C	X
L	W	N	Q	A	H	Q	C	R	V	Q	T	T	E
D	R	E	A	M	S	C	X	X	J	O	W	E	D
Q	J	T	P	C	W	E	B	S	A	V	A	R	M
A	A	A	Z	G	M	N	G	P	H	R	Z	B	I
S	W	P	L	H	G	D	R	F	C	B	V	J	A
N	B	Y	R	O	F	Y	M	Y	S	T	N	R	K

DECISIONS // RETHINK // BEST // TRUST // CHOICES //
LISTEN // IMPATIENT // DREAMS // RULES //
EXCITED // HAPPY // WISE // REMEMBER // CHARACTER

Answer on page 108.

God is always waiting to hear from you and you can speak to Him whenever you have important decisions to make!

Just remember that when you make your plans WITH GOD, 'You can go safely on your way and never even stumble' (Proverbs 3 v 23).

Well, that's number 3 of our Topz 10: God has good plans for you!

Here's a prayer for you to say right now ...

Thank You, my Father God, that You love me so much. Thank You that You are interested in everything I do. Thank You that You have good plans for my life!

While I am making plans or trying to decide something important, please help me to remember You first. To keep You right in the centre of my heart and my thoughts.

I want my plans to be Your plans. Please guide me and teach me to listen to You. Amen.

When you've said the prayer, why not decorate the page around it to help you remember how amazing it is to be able to share your plans with God?

THE BIBLE IS YOUR GUIDE

How much do you think you know about the Bible?
Try this quiz!

1. How many books are there in the Bible?

25 ☐   50 ☐   66 ☐

2. What are the names of the two parts of the Bible?

The Big Part and the Small Part ☐
The Old Testament and the New Testament ☐
The First Bit and the Second Bit ☐

3. What are the four Gospels called?

William, Simon, Philip and Henry ☐
Matthew, Mark, Luke and John ☐
Michael, Richard, Solomon and Cuthbert ☐

4. Which is the very last book in the Bible?

Revelation ☐   Acts ☐   Philippians ☐

5. Which is the very last book in the Old Testament?

Malachi ☐   Daniel ☐   Exodus ☐

6. What type of book is Romans in the New Testament?

A story ☐   A recipe ☐   A letter ☐

7. Who wrote the book of Romans?

Luke ☐   Paul ☐   Noah ☐

8. Who wrote the book of Isaiah in the Old Testament?

Isaiah the prophet ☐
Isaiah the farmer ☐
Isaiah the bank manager ☐

9. How many psalms are there in the book of Psalms?

150 ☐   99 ☐   33 ☐

10. Who is the book of Acts in the New Testament about?

A man called Jim ☐
A group of actors ☐
Jesus' disciples ☐

Answers on page 108.

How many did you get ...?
Well, guess what? Knowing stuff like this is groovy-doovy – but there's SO much more to the Bible than just a bunch of facts!

Try this: breathe in and out five times. BUT –

Don't just do it the way you normally do it – without thinking about it. Because let's face it, most of the time breathing just happens. We breathe in and out, over and over, day after day after day, and don't even notice we're doing it.

So this time, as you breathe in and out, *really* focus on what you're doing. Notice the air filling your lungs as you breathe in. Notice the rush through your nose as you breathe out. Feel your chest going up and down with each breath.

Every breath you take feeds you with vital oxygen.

Your body needs oxygen to live!

EVERY BREATH YOU TAKE FILLS YOU WITH LIFE!

But, what's that got to do with the Bible, you're probably wondering? (OK, you can stop thinking about your breathing now …)

Well, the thing about the Bible is that it's not like any other book on the shelf. Yes, it's full of stories, and some Bibles have pictures in, too. But what makes the Bible different from all your other books is that it's ALIVE!

It's alive with God! God Himself inspired it.

In other words, God made sure it was written by the people He wanted to write it, using the words He wanted them to write.

God breathed His life into the book we call the Bible so that through reading it, we could:

- **Learn all about Him.**

- **Understand how to be friends with Him.**

- **Discover how to live our lives in the way that's best for us – and of course God knows what's best for us because He created us!**

'All Scripture is inspired by God and is useful for teaching the truth ... and giving instruction for right living, so that the person who serves God may be fully qualified and equipped to do every kind of good deed' (2 Timothy 3 v 16–17).

In case you're wondering, 'Scripture' in this verse means the Bible.

THE BIBLE

38

The Bible itself (which is basically God Himself speaking to us) tells us that it's inspired by God!

When we read it, if we ask God to teach us *through our reading*, He will speak to us and breathe His life into us – just as every breath you take into your lungs when you breathe fills you with human life.

GOOD, EH?

Now, you wouldn't forget to breathe, would you? So it's important not to forget to read your Bible either. How about making sure you find time to read a little bit every day? Even just a verse? You see, God didn't mean His Book to be something you look at only when you feel like it.

He didn't fill it with His life so that it could sit in your bookcase and only get taken out when you clean your bedroom.

Which would be about once a year in my case ... or even once every two years ...

Oh, John! No. The Bible was designed by God to teach us how to live our lives as His friends. How to have a loving relationship with Him as our heavenly Father, so that one day we can be with Him forever.

God has breathed life into His Book. And when we choose to read it regularly, we can be filled with that life.

How many Bible stories do you know? Write a list of some that you have read or heard about:

_____

_____

_____

_____

_____

If you have a favourite Bible story, which is it?

_____

_____

_____

_____

_____

Can you explain what the story is trying to teach you?

_____

_____

_____

_____

_____

So, if you ever find yourself wondering what's so special about the Bible, remember that it's God speaking to you. It's His 'Book of Instructions' for the best way to live your life.

Put a tick in each box as each sentence is true!

☐ **It'll give you lots of advice and encouragement**

☐ **It'll remind you that God is always close by**

☐ **It'll teach you to trust in God's promises**

☐ **It'll help you with problems and decisions**

This is all pretty mega-fandabulous – but obviously the Bible can only do any of that for you IF YOU READ IT!

God wants to be your best Friend. He wants to share every day with you.

Do you want to share every day with Him?

Then make sure, before you plan anything else for your day, your week, your month ... that you have set aside time to read His Word (the Bible).

To hear through it what He wants you to hear.

To breathe in His life.

HERE'S A CHALLENGE!

Think about what you have to do each day: school, homework, helping your parents or someone else who looks after you, looking after pets, seeing friends ...

Now decide which time of day is the best for you to spend some quiet moments reading your Bible. Not just every now and then, or once a week perhaps. This is about reading God's Word every single day.

Have you worked out your best time? Write it down here:

_____

And now for the real challenge! You've written down your 'Bible time' – see if you can stick to it. Every day.

Things can happen to interrupt our plans – because that's life and they just do. But when you wake up each morning, try to remember God and then do your best – your *absolute* best – to spend some quiet time with Him.

So that's number 4 of our Topz 10: the Bible is your guide!

Pray this prayer now ...

Dear Lord God, thank You for inspiring the Bible. Help me not to take it for granted or leave it collecting dust on my bookshelf or under my bed. You, the Creator of the universe, want to talk directly to me, and I want to hear You. Please help me get into the habit of reading my Bible every day. Amen.

5

GOD UNDERSTANDS

Jesus did totally amazing things when He lived on earth. Apart from all His brilliant teaching, and the fandabulous miracles He did, He also had this incredibly upbeat attitude to everything.

Jesus worked for His Father – God – day in, day out. He never complained about how much there was to do, or how many people followed Him around needing His help. He never moaned about all the travelling He had to do, even though some days His feet must have felt as if they were dropping off with so much walking. He never sulked because He was tired. He never argued with God and said, 'I just don't feel like it!'

The greatest and most unselfish thing Jesus did was to die for us. For you and for me. He died to take God's punishment for the things we sometimes do wrong. He died so that we could be friends with God forever.

Jesus' death was horrible. There was pain and suffering. There were people who spat at Him and laughed at Him.

But Jesus was obedient to God and **HE NEVER ONCE COMPLAINED**.

Phew! That's a bit of a tall order! Never complaining? Never moaning? Never sulking? Never arguing?

Is it even *possible* for us? After all, Jesus is God's Son. He was a perfect Man. And a perfect God ...

But that's the whole point. Jesus *was* a Man when He lived on earth. **HUMAN LIKE US.** He *would* have had feelings, like us. Things *would* have annoyed Him and made Him sad. His feet *would* have hurt! He *would* have got tired.

Most of all, Jesus would have felt fear. He knew what was going to happen to Him and He would have felt very frightened.

But this was what God had sent Him to earth for: to save everyone. And Jesus chose to obey. He never once said: 'It's not fair! Why me?'

God hopes that, as we get to know Him better and read more of the Bible, we will grow to be more like Jesus. More obedient and more willing to serve Him without making a fuss. But He knows it'll take time. Probably a very long time! He understands how we feel about all sorts of different things. And He's there to help us.

That's right! God knows we get upset. He knows there are days we're unhappy. He knows we argue – John and me, we argue loads! God *knows* – and He wants *us* to know we can go to Him with all of it. Because He understands.

Here are my top ten things that I can get really upset about. Honestly, they can wreck my mood for a whole entire day!

1. Having a row with Sarah (just the worst!).

2. Not understanding *anything* in my maths lesson, so not understanding *anything* of my maths homework (mega worry).

3. One of my parents not being well. Makes me worried and sad.

4. When I catch their bug and feel really ill!

5. Not being able to find something I really want to find! You know when you search and search 'cos it must be *somewhere* but it doesn't seem to be *anywhere*? Grrrr!

6. Not being allowed to watch TV until I've tidied my room (double grrrr!).

7. Getting the blame for doing something I didn't do.

8. Practising my violin really hard, then playing it all wrong at the concert (made me cry).

9. When Sarah lost her cat, Saucy.

10. When anyone's mean to me or one of my friends.

People worry and get upset about all sorts of different things. Like I did, see if you can come up with a list of your top ten things that are real mood-wreckers for you. Write them down here:

1. _____
2. _____
3. _____
4. _____
5. _____
6. _____
7. _____
8. _____
9. _____
10. _____

So, the big question is, when any of these things happens and gets us feeling down, what can we do about it? If we talk to God, will He take us seriously? Or will He just think we need to pull ourselves together?

Think of what you've been learning about God:

He loves you.

He wants to be involved in your life.

He cares about ALL the details.

That doesn't sound like someone who expects you to pull yourself together if you feel upset, does it!

Now think about Jesus and the way He behaved, no matter how much work He had to do, or how tired or scared He was.

Jesus shows us that **WE CAN CHOOSE HOW WE REACT TO THINGS**. Jesus chose to obey God and get on with everything He had to do without making a fuss.

And there are some things (things that can spoil our moods, even though they're very tiny) that we can choose not to make a fuss about, too. Things like being asked to keep our bedrooms tidy. Or getting on with our homework. Or looking after things properly so they don't get lost or broken. These are all things that we might not feel like doing and so we get annoyed about them.

But we could instead look at them as if they're actually quite sensible. Quite helpful and all part of family life. We could cut out the moaning and think, 'Yup, fair enough.' And, like Jesus, we could choose to obey, and not feel grumpy about them.

But there are bigger upsets that sometimes crop up in life – and then it's not so easy.

Does your list of ten things that spoil your good mood include falling out with a friend or worrying about your parents? Or having to cope with someone being mean to you, or something happening to one of your pets?

Sad, upsetting and worrying things do happen. Just because we have God in our lives, unfortunately doesn't mean they won't.

But what it *does* mean is that when we're upset over something – or worried, or even angry – we can go to God and say, **'HELP ME.'** And God will help us. Whatever it is, He'll go through it with us because He understands how we feel. He understands because He felt everything Jesus felt when Jesus lived on earth as a human being.

When you're feeling down, God wants you to go to Him and talk to Him.

It's true! Just look at what the Bible says!

'Don't worry about anything, but in all your prayers ask God for what you need … And God's peace, which is far beyond human understanding, will keep your hearts and minds safe' (Philippians 4 v 6–7).

If you're having a bad time over something, talking it through with other people is great. My dad's brilliant at giving me advice. And I talk to the Gang, too. We always sort of know when something's up with one of us.

When you're upset about something, talking to your friends or your family is a really good idea. Never sit there stewing over something on your own. That can sometimes make a problem seem even bigger than it is! So always share it with someone else. Like John's dad, hopefully they'll have some great advice to help you sort it all out.

And never forget that God is there for you, too.

He is there when no one else understands. He is there when everyone else is too busy.

So talk to Him. You may not be able to see Him, but He is there. **ALWAYS.**

'For God has said, "I will never leave you; I will never abandon you." Let us be bold, then, and say: "The Lord is my helper, I will not be afraid"' (Hebrews 13 v 5–6).

How cool is that! I've learnt those verses by heart to say to myself when I'm worried or upset, or if I feel all on my own. Try it! It really helps!

A few pages ago, you wrote a list of things you get upset about.

Well, it's time to look at the flip side! Here are my top ten things that make me happy!

1. Having a best friend who's as super-snazzy as Sarah!

2. Being in the Topz Gang.

3. Knowing God's on my side!

4. Living in Holly Hill – because as towns go, it's actually pretty groovy.

5. Being able to play the violin – even though I mess it up sometimes.

6. Playing sport – just love it!

7. Going away on holiday with Mum and Dad.

8. Free weekends to do stuff with Sarah.

9. Imagining all the different things I could be when I grow up!

10. Being outdoors – SO love summertime!

Your turn! What puts a huge grin on your face?
What are your top ten things that make you want to
laugh out loud?

1. _____
2. _____
3. _____
4. _____
5. _____
6. _____
7. _____
8. _____
9. _____
10. _____

Isn't it fantastic to have
things to giggle about –
get excited about – leap up
and down about! I do lots
of leaping! I sing when I'm
happy, too!

Haha! So much leaping and singing!

When it comes down to it though, we're probably not likely to feel *that* happy all the time – that 'leaping about singing' sort of happy.

But God knows that, and it's all right.

Because you know what? Jesus experienced ups and downs, too, but through it all He had one thing that never changed – God's peace.

Whatever is going on with you, happy things or sad and upsetting things, you can still have that same peace! It's a feeling deep inside you that says, 'It's OK, it's going to be good in the end, God will make sure of it.'

So if you're wondering, 'Does God understand how I feel right now?'

Yes, oh yes, He does!

And that's number 5 of our Topz 10:
God understands!

How brilliant is that! Here's a prayer for you to say …

Sometimes, God, I don't like how I feel. Something might happen to upset me and make me sad. Or nothing might happen at all, but somehow I just feel down and grumpy. And sometimes I don't really understand my own feelings, so how can I even talk about them? But You understand, God. You know how I feel because Jesus lived on earth and had feelings, too. And You listen to me. You see right inside me. Please help me to remember that I can come to You with everything. Absolutely everything. Amen.

Do you love chatting? It's fun, isn't it?

When you chat to your friends, you can make each other laugh, help each other out, share ideas, make plans, mess about and get to know each other better. (Who knew that Josie likes chomping on raw carrots?!)

Who do you really enjoy chatting to?

_____

_____

What do you like to talk about?

_____

_____

_____

_____

What do you like best about chatting to your friends?

_____

_____

_____

_____

Hello

Well, did you know that God, your Father in heaven and your very best Friend, wants you to talk to Him just the way you talk to all your other friends? He really does!

You see, talking to God – praying to Him – is a vital (and really cool!) part of your friendship with Him.

After all, if you didn't talk to your friends and they didn't talk to you, it wouldn't say much for your friendships, would it?

Spending time talking to God helps to keep you close to Him, and helps you get to know Him, too. It builds your friendship with Him and makes it strong. It will help you to know that God is right beside you **EVERY MOMENT OF EVERY DAY.**

Talking to your family and chatting with your friends can be brilliant times. Moments spent chatting with God can be fantastic and exciting and comforting, too!

The Bible tells us to pray. And when God hears us speaking to Him, He's right there with His ears – and His arms – open.

'Come near to God, and he will come near to you' (James 4 v 8).

Even if sometimes it doesn't feel like it to you, God is always there. Hoping you'll chat to Him. Ready to listen.

How often do you chat to God? (Tick your answer!)

Every day ☐

Once or twice a week ☐

Sometimes ☐

When I remember ☐

Not sure ☐

How often do you think God *would like you* to chat to Him? (Tick your answer!)

Every day ☐

Once or twice a week ☐

Sometimes ☐

When I remember ☐

Not sure ☐

If you ticked 'Every day', give yourself a HUGE round of applause!

It's not that God says: 'If you don't talk to me every day, I won't bother to listen!' Definitely not! God always listens. But He wants you to talk to Him as much as possible – every day, as many times a day as you want – so that your friendship with Him will grow and grow. The more time you spend with God, the more He can show you how much He loves you, and how much you can trust Him and depend on Him.

If you have a friend you don't see or talk to anymore – maybe they've moved away or go to a different school now – it affects your friendship. You don't feel so close to them. It's the same with God. Talking to Him regularly and often keeps you close, and helps you to understand what an amazing Friend He is to you.

Praying to God can simply mean having a chat and telling Him about all the stuff that's going on in your life. But remembering to include the following things in your prayers is important, too. Trace over the letters to read what they are:

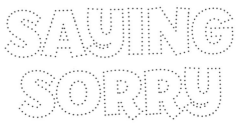

for anything you may have done wrong.

ASKING

for help or for something you or someone else needs.

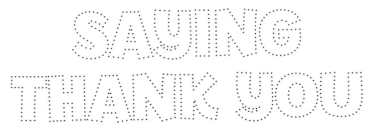

for all the good things God has given you.

1. SAYING SORRY

I told a lie the other day. I had homework due in and I totally forgot to do it! So ... I made up an excuse that wasn't true. It got me out of trouble but afterwards I felt so bad. I didn't want to pray that night, but I did anyway. I said sorry to God and, you know what, I felt so much better afterwards! I knew that God had forgiven me. I don't want to tell lies like that again!

Sometimes we do things we know God wouldn't like – like being selfish, telling a lie or saying something unkind about someone. The Bible calls these sort of things 'sin', and sin can get in the way of our friendship with God and make it hard to feel close to Him.

But God wants to help us! Because – did you know? – God can forgive these things and give us a brand-new start! A shiny-bright, fresh-as-a-daisy, completely clean life again!

So the next time you feel bad about something you've done, don't try to hide it from God. That can only make matters worse! Instead, go to God and talk to Him. And if you say sorry – and really mean it – God will forgive you **COMPLETELY**! He loves you *so* much and He wants you to get the absolute best out of the life He has given you.

2. ASKING

The Bible has lots of stories about people who prayed to God, asking for something in particular. Whether they needed help or protection or basic things like food, God listened and looked after them.

And there's nothing wrong with asking God for things, especially when we *need* them. But God also loves to give us good things that we *don't* necessarily need! Just like a dad might give presents to his children, God enjoys giving us gifts because it's a way of showing His love for us.

There's a very famous king who's written about in the Old Testament of the Bible. He knew how important it was to talk to God. His name was Solomon. He loved God, and God loved him. So one day, God asked Solomon what he would like as a present.

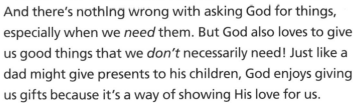

Can you imagine? GOD asked Solomon, 'What would you like me to give you?' (1 Kings 3 v 5) Whew!! I mean, what would YOU have asked for?

But all Solomon wanted was to serve God and to be a good king. So he asked for wisdom. And because he'd asked for such a good thing – not for something selfish or greedy, but something that would help him to help other people – God gave it to him. Straightaway.

God answered: 'I will give you more wisdom and understanding than anyone has ever had before or will ever have again' (1 Kings 3 v 12).

Is there something you'd like God to do for you at the moment? If there is, why not write a prayer to Him? Use the space here. As you write your prayer, remember that God wants the very best for you. Think about how much He loves you and let Him guide you as you talk to Him.

We can also ask God to help others. We can ask Him for things *for them* – especially if they don't know God themselves. Do you know any people who need God's help and comfort at the moment? It might be friends or family, or perhaps people you've heard about in the news recently who are going through sad times.

Use this page to write down the names of some people you could pray for. If you can't think of anyone right now, write a name down when you next hear of someone, to remind you to talk to God about them. Then write a prayer.

Don't forget – God hears everyone who talks to Him. God hears YOU.

3. SAYING THANK YOU

God is good! So good in fact that we will never run out of things we can be thankful for!

So it's time to get thinking – and thanking!

Think of all the things and people in your life that you can thank God for.

Think of everything about YOURSELF you can thank God for – things you're good at, fab things about your personality.

Think of all the times you've asked for something and God has answered you – maybe you needed His help with understanding some tricky work at school, or you asked Him to be close to you when you felt nervous or scared about something.

Now, use the space on the next page to write a prayer. Say thank You, and ask God to help you remember every day just how important you are to Him. And if ever you feel down about yourself in the future, or just need help remembering what to be thankful for, dig out this book and read your prayer through, speaking it out to God! What are you waiting for? Get writing!

I'm always thanking God for food! I *love* food! Hey! Why not colour in this *Thank You* page to make it really stand out?!

God wants us to talk to Him about anything and everything. He wants to share our happy things. He wants to help us when stuff is difficult.

He wants to know when we're sorry, and when we need or want something.

And He *loves* to hear us say thank You!

God NEVER ignores our prayers.

He ALWAYS listens.

He ALWAYS hears.

And He ALWAYS answers.

So that's number 6 of our Topz 10: you can talk to God!

Why not talk to Him RIGHT NOW with this prayer …

Dear Father, thank You for being a God who cares and listens. I want to talk to You more and more. Please remind me that You are always there and that You hear every word I speak. You are the best Friend anyone could ever have. Thank You, God. Amen.

7 YOU CAN TRUST GOD

Just like talking to God, there's something else God hopes will help you when things get tricky. And that is **TRUST**.

Jesus is a perfect example of trust in God.

Jesus chose to obey God and do what God wanted Him to do. And He was totally sure that God was backing Him up all the way.

Jesus never doubted that God loved Him. He never doubted that God would be there to help Him through.

It was because Jesus trusted God so completely that He was able to feel peace and have such an incredible attitude to life and work. Jesus knew God was always there for Him and that would never change. **DO YOU KNOW IT, TOO?**

When you think about 'trusting' someone, what does that mean to you?

See if you can write down here *how* you trust someone else, and what sorts of things you can trust them with.

_____

_____

_____

_____

_____

_____

_____

_____

What did you come up with? Trusting someone to me means that I feel I can talk to that person about *anything*. I feel I can tell them my secrets and not worry that they'll go and tell someone else. I can be upset and know they won't think I'm just being stupid. I can count on them to help me out when I really need them. I feel safe when I'm around them because I know that whatever happens, they'll always be *for* me, not against me.

Trust is something that gets stronger and stronger the more we *know* the person we trust! Well, there are plenty of ways to get to know God. Fill in the missing letters and see!

R _ _ _ in_ t_e B_ _le

_al_ _n_ t_ H_ _

L_ _te_ _ _ _ _o _i_

Ta_ _i_ _ and li_ _ _ni_ _

to ot _ _ r C_ _is_ i _ ns

Answers on page 109.

In number *6* of our ***TOPZ 10***, we thought about how we can talk to God. We learnt that He's *always* listening! But what about when He doesn't seem to be answering? Does that mean He's not trustworthy?

No! God is COMPLETELY trustworthy! The Bible says so! 'God keeps every promise he makes' (Proverbs 30 v 5). So if you're waiting for an answer to a prayer and starting to think that God's taking no notice, it might be that He has answered already – but perhaps with a **NO** or a **NOT JUST YET**.

So, why might God be saying, 'No' to a prayer?

God wants to give us good things. He wants to take care of us and make sure we have what we need. But what if we ask God for something that's just plain bad for us?

Dear God, You know how much I like chocolate? Well, could You please make sure that I have a lifetime supply of milk chocolate, and lots of it – starting today? Amen.

Hmmm ... what do you think God's answer will be? Write it in the box.

Sometimes what's good and bad for us may not be as obvious as too much chocolate. But God made us. He knows us inside out. What's bad for us and what's good. And He loves us. So, if you ask God for something and nothing happens, it's not because He's ignoring you. It's more than likely He's got a very good reason for saying, 'No'.

What if God says, 'Not yet'?

Do you think you're a patient sort of person?

I'm not! Mum's always saying, 'Just wait!' or, 'What's the hurry?' or, 'Stop wishing your life away!' That's just me, I suppose. The most impatient person in a whole world full of impatient people! When I want something, I want it NOW: my birthday, chocolate, new shoes, the end of term. Sometimes I want it to be Christmas NOW and it's only – like – March ...

Well, it can be like that with prayer, too.

You've asked God *for* something, or *to do* something, or *to show you* something. You think, 'Great!' and you expect it to happen. NOW. But even though you wait ...

And wait ...

And wait ...

Nothing seems to change.

You ask God again, maybe. You wait again. Still nothing. At least that's the way it seems ... *HELLO ...?*

IS THERE ANYONE THERE?

Well, yes. There is someone there. God's there. Right there. So why don't you get exactly what you want exactly when you want it?

If God seems to be answering one of your prayers with 'not yet', it might be because He's trying to TEACH you something. After all, **IT TAKES TIME** to learn things, doesn't it?

How old are you?

_____

How many years have you been at school?

_____

How old were you when you learned to talk (ask someone who knew you as a baby)?

_____

How old were you when you could spell your name?

_____

Have you ever stopped to think how much you know? You've been learning since the day you were born! We all have.

You learn things at home: how to wash, brush your teeth, get dressed, and talk. You might start to learn the alphabet, and to read and write, too.

Then, when you go to school, you learn a whole heap more! Reading, writing, how numbers work, science stuff, history – maybe even a different language. You discover what you like and what you don't like. You find out loads about yourself and other people!

So maybe God is answering with 'not just yet' because He knows you need a bit more time to learn something.

Also, did you know that the way God sees time is totally different from the way we see time?!

'A thousand years to you are like one day' (Psalm 90 v 4).

Woah! How can a thousand years *ever* be like a day? But the Bible tells us that to God, that's the way it is.

Now, we can't understand the way God thinks. We can't see things the way God sees them. Because God is God. All powerful. All knowing. Everlasting! And we're only human.

We just have to trust Him. Trust that He knows what's best for us.

God's timing isn't always going to fit in with what we want. After all, He sees so much more than right now, and tomorrow, and next week, and next year. He sees the next thousand years! And the thousand years after that! He knows where we fit and when is the best time for everything.

So trust me when I say, **YOU REALLY CAN TRUST GOD**!

Here are three Topz tips for trusting God when you're waiting for your prayers to be answered:

1. **Be patient.** Remember, God may be trying to teach you something, even if it's just patience.

2. **Be thankful** for what you already have. God is so good to us!

3. **Keep going!** Don't ever stop talking to God. Don't give up.

God knows you better than anyone because He is with you every minute of every day.

You can tell Him anything – be totally 100 per cent YOURSELF – and nothing will ever change the way He feels about you.

And that's number 7 of our Topz 10:
you can trust God!

Why not write a prayer here now, perhaps asking God *for* something you or someone else needs, or *to do* something, or *to show you* something. Then, as you speak it out, finish it with the words below:

_____

_____

_____

_____

_____

_____

_____

_____

Thank You for listening, Lord God. Please help me to be patient and to wait for Your perfect timing. I trust You. Amen.

YOU ARE A TEMPLE

I bet you've never been called a 'temple' before? Haha! But you are! The Bible says so!

'Don't you know that your body is the temple of the Holy Spirit, who lives in you and who was given to you by God?' (1 Corinthians 6 v 19).

But **WHAT** does that mean exactly? Well, guess what? Number **8** of our **TOPZ 10** is all about YOU! You see, thinking about yourself is important. Yes, it's good to think about other people. But never forget that YOU matter, too. God made you and you're very special to Him.

So special, that when you give your life over to Him and then ask Him to, He'll send His Holy Spirit to come and live inside you.

The Holy Spirit is **GOD LIVING IN YOU**! Wow! And the Holy Spirit will help you every day to:

- **Live the way God wants you to**

- **Make careful choices and decisions**

- **Feel close to God.**

I know! Super snazzy!

Our house is really clean. I mean, really, *really* clean. That's not a bad thing. It's just that Mum is mega house proud. She likes it all sparkly all day every day, in case anyone pops in. I s'pose I kind of get it – I like to keep my bike all clean and sparkly. People notice, too. When I'm out cycling, they say things like, 'Wow! Your bike is so clean and sparkly!' Not quite so on it with my bedroom though ...

How about you? If you've got a friend coming round, do you tidy your room before they see it? Or at least make sure you haven't left your dirty socks lying about?

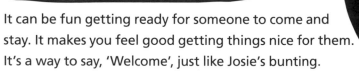

When my cousin comes to stay, I always get my room ready. I make sure it's clean and tidy, and last time I hung up some bunting that said 'Welcome'!

It can be fun getting ready for someone to come and stay. It makes you feel good getting things nice for them. It's a way to say, 'Welcome', just like Josie's bunting.

So, think about it – God wants to send His Holy Spirit – who, like Jesus, is also God – to live inside you. Doesn't His Spirit deserve a big welcome? Yes, He does! God gave you your body and you owe it to Him and to His Holy Spirit to look after it, so it's a fit place for the Spirit to come and live in.

You owe it to YOURSELF to look after yourself too! To grow up into the best, happiest and healthiest person you can possibly be – and you can help yourself to do that by caring for yourself. Starting right now!

Have a think first about **WHAT YOU EAT**!

Here's a bit of a test for you. Let's find out how healthily you eat by ticking the sentence that most describes you for each of the following choices:

☐ **A.** I eat chips whenever I can.

☐ **B.** I like chips sometimes, but I also like ordinary potatoes.

☐ **A.** If there's fruit or ice cream for pudding, I always choose ice cream.

☐ **B.** I like ice cream sometimes, but I eat lots of fruit too.

☐ **A.** Crisps are my favourite snack.

☐ **B.** I like crisps sometimes but I often snack on raisins or raw veggies.

☐ **A.** When I'm thirsty, I always go for fizzy drinks.

☐ **B.** I like a fizzy drink sometimes, but I drink lots of water too.

☐ **A.** Sometimes I'm so hungry when I get home from school, I eat loads of biscuits – especially the chocolate ones!

☐ **B.** When I'm really hungry, I might eat a couple of biscuits, but a banana is really good too.

☐ **A.** I eat sweets nearly every day.

☐ **B.** I usually only eat sweets about once a week – or as a special treat.

☐ **A.** I like chocolatey breakfast cereal with extra sugar every morning.

☐ **B.** I enjoy chocolatey cereal, but I don't eat it every day. Often I have porridge or muesli.

Now, add up how many 'A's and how many 'B's you ticked!

Number of 'A's ☐

Number of 'B's ☐

If you ticked mostly 'B's – hooray hoorah! You're already eating a lot of good, healthy food. If you ticked mostly 'A's, you might want to start thinking about how to have a healthier diet!

Dad did this thing once. Our car runs on petrol, and one day he was in a hurry and accidentally put diesel in it. Oops. So it stopped working. And Dad ended up even later than he was already. He was seriously not happy.

God designed us to need fuel – food. The 'right fuel' is good, healthy food, which is what helps us to grow, have strong bones and all our inside bits working the way they should.

In Genesis, the very first book in the Bible, God says:

'I have provided all kinds of grain and all kinds of fruit for you to eat' (Genesis 1 v 29).

You see, God made us. So He knows how we work, and what makes us work best. Which is why He gave us the right sort of food to eat, and the means to grow it for ourselves.

And God always knows what He's doing! If we eat food that isn't good for us too often, the chances are we won't be as fit and healthy as we could be. We might not be able to concentrate so well. We might not have so much energy. Remember the petrol car with a tank full of diesel ... Phuttt!

TIME FOR SOME FOOD FUN!

Eating healthily doesn't have to be boring.
So here's a challenge for you! Can you design yourself a REALLY HEALTHY and REALLY EXCITING packed lunch? On the next page is a lunchbox for you to fill. Why not think of things you've never tried before? Just remember to stick to what's good for you:

- **Lots of fruit and vegetables**

- **Wholegrain bread, rice or pasta**

- **Not too much fatty food like chips, crisps and pastry**

- **Not too much sugary food like biscuits, cakes, sweets and chocolate**

Trying out new stuff is brilliant. So trying out new FOOD stuff is stonkingly brilliant!

God wants you to make the most of everything He has given you. And looking after yourself properly with a really good diet is a fantastic starting point. Of course, it's fine to have treats every now and then – where would the universe be without chocolate?! Just make sure you don't overdo it, and remember to try to eat a good variety of different foods – which is actually really fun!

LET'S MOVE IT!

Inside you, your heart is working incredibly hard. It beats away, pumping your blood around your body day and night to keep you alive – and most of the time, you don't even think about it!

So, just as you (should!) brush your teeth regularly so that you don't get tooth decay, and shower or bath regularly to help keep your skin clean and in good condition, so you should also remember your heart and check that you're looking after it as well as you can.

One of the most important ways to be kind to your heart is to get plenty of exercise.

Sitting in front of the computer or the TV for hours on end won't do a lot for your heart! It won't give it the bursts of activity it needs to keep it fit and strong.

When you run and jump about, you get out of breath, don't you? And when you're out of breath, your heart pumps faster. So not only are you giving *yourself* a workout – you're giving your heart a workout, too! You're making sure your heart gets the exercise it needs to keep on pumping! To keep itself and you healthy.

How many hours do you spend watching TV or playing on the computer each day?

_____

How many hours do you spend doing some exercise each day?

_____

I love to move – it's keeping still I'm not so good at!

Danny's a proper sports freak. He's mad for anything that gets him moving and running about.

Danny's favourite class at school: PE
Danny's hobbies: football, cycling, jogging, swimming

See what I mean? A PROPER sports freak!

Getting enough exercise is just as important as eating plenty of the right foods when it comes to keeping as healthy as possible. And exercise isn't just good for your heart. It's good for THE WHOLE of you!

If you're like Danny and you love sport, then doing exercise will be a part of your life because it's your 'thing'. What you really enjoy. But if you're someone who finds sport a bit of a drag – who sees PE on your school timetable and thinks, 'Moan! Groan!' – keeping fit might seem like a bit of an uphill struggle.

Don't despair! Getting exercise isn't all bad news! And you don't need to spend hours and hours a day exercising. Getting enough rest is important, too.

If you enjoy football like Danny, then groovy-doovy. Josie loves it, too. Team sports are great. So are things you can do on your own like jogging and cycling. But if you're just not sporty (like me!) there are other ways to keep fit. You've just got to find something fun that you really like to do!

Here are a few ideas for you:

- **Play your favourite music and have a good dance about!**

- **Find a friend and have a hopping race!**

- **Skip with a skipping rope for five minutes and count how many skips you do!**

- **Run on the spot for five minutes – do ten running steps slowly, then ten running steps super-fast, then back to ten slowly and so on. After five minutes have a five-minute rest, then do it again!**

- **Lie down on the floor and circle your legs in the air as if you're riding a bike!**

- **Go for a good walk with your family or friends, stepping out fast enough to get your heart pumping!**

Cool!

A CHALLENGE FOR YOU!

Starting from next Monday (Monday is always a great day to start something new!), write down below what activity you are going to do each day of the week to help keep you and your heart in *TIP-TOPZ* condition. You can include school PE sessions if you want to. Or get creative and plan out your own exercise routines. Did you know you can even exercise sitting down? Try sitting and punching your arms quickly into the air for five minutes and see how out of breath you get! Anything you want to do even for five or ten minutes a day is brilliant!

Monday _____

Tuesday _____

Wednesday _____

Thursday _____

Friday _____

Saturday _____

Sunday _____

Got your plan? Now for the biggest challenge of all – see if for one whole week you can STICK TO IT!

When I think about me, often I find myself thinking about God, too. Do you know why? Because God made me. I want to do my best to keep myself fit and healthy because – well – I want to be fit and healthy! But also because it's a way to say thank You to God for putting me all together.

When someone gives you a present that you totally *love*, you want to take care of it, don't you? You want it to last and last so that you can enjoy it day after day.

It should be like that with our bodies, too. We should be thankful to God for them – they are a present! And we should care for them as a step towards making them a great place for His Holy Spirit to come and live inside!

So, that's number 8 of our Topz 10: you are a temple!

Why not say this prayer now ...

Dear Father God, You have made everyone different. We all have different bodies, with different things we're good at and different things we don't find so easy to do. For some people, even ordinary, everyday things can be tricky. But thank You for my body, Father. I want to look after it carefully every day. It's an amazing present to me. I ask the Holy Spirit to come and fill it now. Amen.

9 YOU CAN CHOOSE

Whenever I go out – to the park, to the shops, even to get the bus for school – d'you know what Mum always says? 'Mind the road!'

> My mum always says that, too! What does that even mean – 'Mind the road'? It's not as if the road's going to jump up and eat you, is it? Why don't grown-ups say what they really mean – 'Mind the traffic'!

Do you get told to mind the road (or the traffic!)? How to be careful when you're walking beside or crossing a road is probably one of the first things you were taught when you were little.

And you know why, don't you?

To keep you (trace over the letters) …

It's the same with rules. 'You must do this …
You mustn't do that …' You might think some rules
are stupid. They stop you having fun; stop you doing
what you want to do.

But actually they are probably there for your own good.
To keep you safe.
Think about the people who look after you.

Who looks after you at home?

_____

Who looks after you at school or church?

_____

It may seem as though these people spend a lot of
time making rules and telling you what to do, but it's
because they care about you. They are the people who
want what's best for you.

The people who want to see you make the most of
yourself and your life.

The Bible tells us to respect and obey our parents, or those caring for us.

'My child, pay attention to what your father and mother tell you' (Proverbs 1 v 8).

'Children, it is your Christian duty to obey your parents always, for that is what pleases God' (Colossians 3 v 20).

It doesn't please God because He wants to spoil anyone's fun. It pleases God because He knows that, as we grow up, we need people to take care of us. People to guide us and to teach us.

And if you think it's just children the Bible has advice for, think again! There are important words for grown-ups, too!

'Parents ... raise [your children] with Christian discipline and instruction' (Ephesians 6 v 4).

'Teach children how they should live, and they will remember it all their life' (Proverbs 22 v 6).

You see, God wants the people who look after you and teach you – who have 'authority' over you – to respect Him and obey Him, just as much as He wants you to respect and obey those people! He hopes they will help you to grow up knowing Him and obeying Him.

As you can see, respect and obedience are **BIG THINGS** in the Bible!

Look at these words. They are all things God wants you to learn how to be as you grow up respecting the people around you, and being obedient to Him by living your life the way the Bible tells you to:

KIND // GENEROUS // LOVING // HONEST // UNSELFISH // HARDWORKING // THOUGHTFUL // CARING // HELPFUL // FORGIVING // PATIENT // GENTLE

Can you find them all in the word search?

L	U	F	P	L	E	H	T	G	G	K	Q	F	K
B	T	M	V	W	W	S	W	N	N	I	O	O	B
U	D	N	T	A	E	X	G	I	I	N	D	R	G
C	N	Z	E	N	H	E	X	K	V	D	Z	G	A
K	E	S	O	I	N	U	Y	R	O	W	O	I	Q
V	G	H	E	E	T	J	W	O	L	Q	L	V	Q
Q	P	E	R	L	X	A	P	W	C	N	K	I	O
A	Q	O	N	O	F	X	P	D	B	R	O	N	X
D	U	D	A	T	V	I	L	R	G	W	E	G	H
S	R	H	G	H	L	V	S	A	G	E	F	J	F
U	H	V	W	Y	Q	E	P	H	K	G	H	B	U
T	H	O	U	G	H	T	F	U	L	U	U	G	L
H	Y	H	H	H	U	M	P	V	Z	P	P	I	F
C	A	R	I	N	G	B	B	N	Y	Y	F	Y	P

Answer on page 109.

Well? Did you find all those words? Wow! That's a lot of things God hopes we'll learn to be!

But how about this? They are all things we can **CHOOSE** to be – because living God's way is a **CHOICE**.

When we really love someone, we want to make them happy. Maybe do something kind for them, or give them a present.

When we really love *God*, we'll want to please Him, too. We'll *want* to respect and obey Him because that's what He asks us to do. We'll understand that all He wants is what is best for us.

And, guess what? We have the best Teacher and the best Friend ever to help us choose to respect and obey – God!

Yeah, and here's the coolest bit – the more we love, respect and obey God, and choose to live the way the Bible tells us to, the more God will help us to be all those things in the word search! And the more we'll WANT to be all those things in the word search, because it makes God happy! We'll find it easier to respect those around us, too. Great, huh?!

In the Old Testament is the story of a woman called Hannah.

Oh, yeah, ultra cool story! Hannah was obedient to God in a spectacular way!

She was! But at the start of her story, Hannah was very unhappy. What she wanted more than anything in the world was to have a baby. But it just didn't seem to happen.

So, did Hannah turn her back on God because He hadn't given her what she wanted? Did she decide never to bother talking to Him again?

NO! She still obeyed Him by continuing to worship and pray to Him. She still spoke to Him very respectfully, no matter how miserable she was:

'Almighty LORD, look at me, your servant! See my trouble and remember me! Don't forget me! If you give me a son, I promise that I will dedicate him to you for his whole life' (1 Samuel 1 v 11).

Hannah didn't give up praying to God. She *didn't give up on* God.

Which reminds us of number **7** in our **TOPZ 10**: you can trust God!

And at last, God gave Hannah the baby boy she had asked for, and she called him Samuel.

Hannah obeyed God by staying close to Him, even though she must have felt at times that He wasn't listening to her. And God answered her prayer.

But that wasn't the end of it. Look at Hannah's prayer again.

What did Hannah make to God (fill in the letters)?

A p _ _ _ _ _ _

If God would only give her a son, Hannah had promised that she would give the boy back to Him, so that he could spend his life working for Him.

But when the time came, could she really do it?

Yes, she could. When Samuel was old enough, Hannah took him to a place called Shiloh, a long way from their home, to work for God with a priest called Eli.

Leaving Samuel behind must have been almost impossible to do. Hannah could only visit him once a year. But she had made a promise to God. She kept that promise because she was obedient to God and respected Him.

And guess what? God saw how Hannah was determined to stick with Him, even though letting Samuel go must have been the hardest thing she had ever done. So He gave her more children. Not just one or two – but five! Two daughters and three more sons.

What Hannah had to do was *really* tough. But she chose to trust God and obey Him by keeping her promise.

It's easy to choose to do the things we want to do. Like every year, I decide to write a birthday and a Christmas list – so people know what I want! But it's much harder to decide to do something that may not be easy or fun.

To show God that you're serious about obeying Him and living the way He tells us to in the Bible, are there some kind, helpful, unselfish things you could choose to do for your family or friends? See what you can come up with and write a list here:

_____

_____

_____

_____

_____

_____

_____

_____

_____

Now try to stick to doing the things you've decided to do – and show God you mean business!

God's way of doing things is different to the way many of our friends or neighbours or teachers may do things. We might be so used to **NOT** living God's way that it seems too hard to change. Or we may have made so many mistakes that we think, 'What's the use?'

But the great news is, if we *choose* or *decide* to change, God will give us everything we need to do just that! We are not alone!

Not only that, but God can forgive any mistake and 'wipe the slate clean' for us. The past is the past to Him, so we don't need to feel bad about it.

If you want to say sorry for things you may have done in the past, and if you want God to wash those things away so you can have a brand-new life with Him, here's what you can do:

Go to Him and (trace over the letters) ...

Tell God you're very sorry and ask Him to forgive you.

Then believe that He *has* forgiven you!

So, things to remember:

- **God's rules are not there to spoil your fun**
- **God's rules will help you be the best you can be**
- **God's rules will teach you to be kind and respectful to others so that they can see Him in you!**

Remember, too, that following God is a choice. It's up to you.

But when you do make up your mind to be obedient to Him, then you can snuggle up with your heavenly Father, anywhere, anytime, to have a chat and ask Him to help you. Why not start now? Write down which of God's rules you find hard to obey and talk to Him about what you find difficult.

_____

_____

And that's number 9 of our Topz 10: you can choose!

If you want to follow God, His ways and His plan for your life, then pray this prayer ...

Dear Lord God, thank You for being such a loving and forgiving Father. Teach me to see that You want the best for me and please help me to stay obedient to You – and obedient and respectful to others, too. Amen.

10

YOU WERE MADE TO WORSHIP

When God created the world, His great plan was to build something perfect and beautiful. A completely, perfectly beautiful universe.

But the people He made to live there spoilt things. You see, they were created to love, to worship, but they decided to love other things rather than God. They turned their backs on Him and started doing what *they* wanted to do, rather than what God wanted them to do.

So God's universe wasn't perfect anymore and people's friendship with Him was broken.

But Jesus, God's only Son, came to earth to teach us about God. Jesus came to earth to take God's punishment – the one that we deserve for the wrong things we do.

Jesus died for us.

God gave up His *only* Son so that we could be His friends again.

'For God loved the world so much that he gave his only Son, so that everyone who believes in him may not die but have eternal life' (John 3 v 16).

That verse from the Bible is really famous. And it tells us just how much God really does love us. You and me.

God's love for us is huge. MASSIVE! He loves us way more than Benny loves food and Benny loves food a *lot*!

So if God loves us that much, doesn't He deserve all *our* love, too?

Think about someone close to you who really loves you, takes care of you and spends time with you. Maybe one of your parents or someone else who looks after you. Even a big sister or brother. If you wanted to show them how happy they make you and how much you appreciate what they do for you, what could you do for them?

See what ideas you can come up with and write them down here:

_____

_____

_____

_____

_____

_____

_____

_____

How did you get on? Did you write down some practical things like taking your special person breakfast in bed? Or doing the hoovering all round the house to be helpful?

Or maybe you thought it would be a brilliant idea to make a special greetings card with a message inside that says: **THANK YOU SO MUCH FOR EVERYTHING!**

Fab idea! I'm definitely going to add that to *my* list!

There really are plenty of ways to do something nice for the people who love you.

But what can you do for God when popping in to surprise Him with a cup of tea and a biscuit isn't really an option?! How can you show Him how truly grateful you are for everything He has done for you? How can you let Him know that you love Him?

So, we've each come up with a funky way for you to show God how special He is to you. That's seven ways to show your love to God and keep your friendship with Him in **TIP-TOPZ** condition at the same time! You'll find a big letter on each of the next few pages, too, for you to colour in and decorate. Read through our ideas and colour in all seven letters. Then sort the letters into the right order to find out the word that sums this all up!

1. MAKE GOD YOUR NUMBER ONE

Good start, huh? It's really easy to remember ... What's number 1 in the list of things to show God you love Him? Oh yeah! Make Him your Number One!

Making God your Number One means putting Him first. Your favourite TV programme might be about to start, but have you talked to God yet today? Have you read your Bible to see if there's something He wants to teach you? Something He really wants to say to you?

Don't wait till you're in bed for the night, and then fall asleep over your prayers! God has given us hours and hours and *hours* of time! So make a space in each day to spend properly with Him. God deserves your wide-awake time, not your sleepy time.

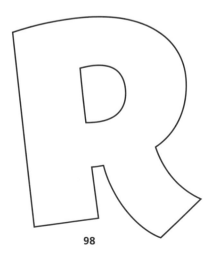

2. DON'T TAKE GOD FOR GRANTED

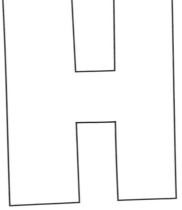

It's so easy to take God for granted! I'm always doing it. When I get a snack from the cupboard at home, I hardly ever stop to think, 'Wow! There's always enough food in this cupboard. I never have to go hungry – thank You, God.' Or when I get home from school, I don't think I've ever said, 'Thank You, God, that I have a house to come home to.' But I SHOULD! Because God has given me so much.

What are you thankful to God for? Write a few things down here. And don't just thank God right now – thank Him every single day. Don't take Him for granted!

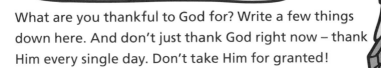

3. LET GOD IN

If your best friend called round with a really cool present for you, you wouldn't say 'no thanks' and tell them to go away – would you? Of course you wouldn't! You'd let them in. Well, God wants us to let Him into our lives so that He can give us the *coolest* present of all time – a life forever with Him as our best Friend.

God wants us to invite Him into every part of our lives. To be involved in what we do day in, day out. Then He can guide us and look after us – day in, day out.

And let's face it, you don't show someone you love them by shutting the door in their face. You show it by opening it up wide and saying, 'Hey! Fantastic to see you, come on in!'

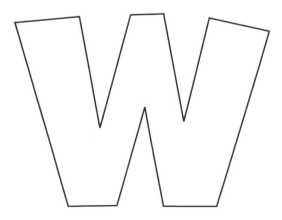

4. SERVE LIKE JESUS

Jesus is the Son of God. He is the greatest and most important Man who ever lived. A King! But God sent Him here to be a Servant. God wants us to be like Jesus. So to show Him that we care about what He wants, we should learn to serve each other like Jesus did.

Jesus had so much power – God's power! But He only ever used it to help other people and to do God's work. He didn't act proud like a king. He acted as a servant. Once, He even crouched down on the floor and washed His disciples' dirty feet. Then He said, 'I have set an example for you' (John 13 v 15).

God wants us to follow Jesus' example – to serve each other by doing good, kind things and helping each other out. And whenever we obey God and do that, we're showing Him we love Him.

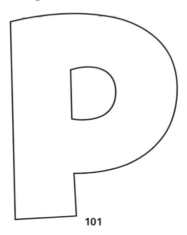

5. STICK TO GOD'S RULES

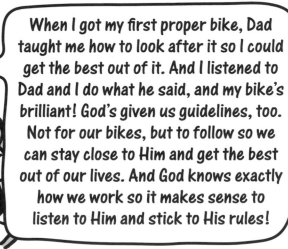

When I got my first proper bike, Dad taught me how to look after it so I could get the best out of it. And I listened to Dad and I do what he said, and my bike's brilliant! God's given us guidelines, too. Not for our bikes, but to follow so we can stay close to Him and get the best out of our lives. And God knows exactly how we work so it makes sense to listen to Him and stick to His rules!

God didn't make rules because He's mean and grumpy. He made rules because He loves us and He really does know what's best for us.

Let's stick to what He teaches us. Respecting God's rules is another way to show Him you love Him.

6. TELL GOD YOU'RE SORRY

You know what it's like if you have a fight with someone. You can end up feeling just awful. If I ever fall out with Josie, it feels like just the worst time ever in the history of worst times. And do you know what the *best* time feels like? When we say sorry and make up! So that's why telling God you're sorry is SO important if you've done something to make Him sad. It shows Him how much you love Him and want everything to be all right again.

Just like arguing with someone spoils your friendship with them, doing things that make God sad gets in the way of your friendship with *Him*, too.

So check on how you feel inside. Is there something you know you need to put right with Him? If there is, make sure to tell Him you're sorry. Then KNOW that you're forgiven – and you and God? You'll be the best of friends again!

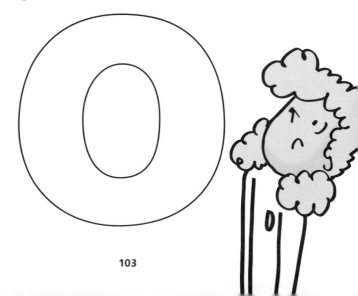

7. NEVER GIVE UP!

When something's really hard, do you ever think, 'Ugh! I can't be bothered!' I get like that with homework sometimes. Especially science. Letting God be in charge of your life can be hard work, too. Sometimes it'll seem way easier to do what *you* want rather than what God wants. But you know what? God is always there for us. He never gives up on us. So let's never give up on Him.

If you want God to see that you mean it when you tell Him you love Him, then keep on going. Keep talking to Him. Keep listening to Him. Keep obeying Him. Keep trying to put Him first.

Hold on to God and He will hold on to you.
No matter what.

'[God's] eternal arms are your support' (Deuteronomy 33 v 27).

So that's it! Seven Topz ways to show God how much He means to you. Seven ways to help you live your life the way God asks you to, knowing that He is right beside you and will never stop loving you and helping you.

HAVE YOU UNJUMBLED ALL THOSE LETTERS YET? Because they spell out the word that sums up all of these things you can do for your Father God. It's a fun thing. An exciting thing. You can get really creative with it, too. And you can give it to God as a gift from you!

When you've worked it out, write it down here:

_____

Yesss! By doing all these things, you can give God your worship!

And you can praise Him in so many different ways! You can sing, dance, clap or worship Him with your prayers. You could even write a song or a poem to sing or speak out to God, telling Him how important He is to you and how much you love Him.

And there's one thing for *absolute* sure: God deserves our love and our worship every single day.

'The Lord's unfailing love and mercy still continue, Fresh as the morning, as sure as the sunrise' (Lamentations 3 v 22–23).

How can you worship God today? Could you make up a song or a dance or a poem?

Or perhaps you could write down why you want to say thank You to Him and why you appreciate everything He has done for you. Then you could read out what you've written to God as a prayer of worship.

HERE IS SOME SPACE FOR YOU TO GET CREATIVE. It's YOUR space to tell God how YOU feel about Him. Have fun worshipping your heavenly Father!

_____

_____

_____

_____

_____

_____

_____

_____

_____

_____

_____

_____

_____

So now you've reached the last one, **number 10 of our Topz 10: you were made to worship God!** And that's not because God is proud and just wants you to tell Him how wonderful He is all the time. It's because He knows that being thankful is *really* good for us! So worshipping God will not only make Him happy, it'll make you happy, too!

And that's it! Our **TOPZ 10** pick of AMAZING things you need to know – and we pray you'll remember them for the rest of your life!

Let's speak to God right now …

Dear Lord God, thank You that You made me, that You love me and that You have great plans for me. Thank You for Jesus and for the Bible. I know they will both guide me and help me. Thank You that I can talk to You and trust You with everything. Help me choose to make the right decisions, and please fill me with Your Holy Spirit and make me strong. Be with me, Father, for the rest of my life on earth – until I see You face to face in heaven! Amen.

ANSWERS

Page 33

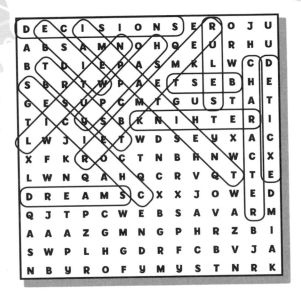

Pages 35–36

1. 66
2. The Old Testament and the New Testament
3. Matthew, Mark, Luke and John
4. Revelation
5. Malachi
6. Letter
7. Paul
8. Isaiah the prophet
9. 150
10. Jesus' disciples

Page 67

Reading the Bible

Talking to Him

Listening to Him

Talking and listening to other Christians

Page 88

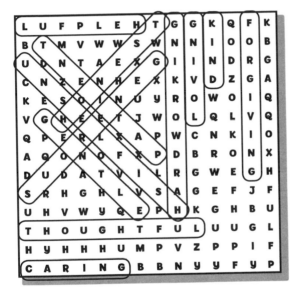

Page 91

A promise

TOPZ EVERY DAY

Topz is an exciting, day-by-day look at the Bible with the Topz Gang! Full of fun activities, word games, puzzles, cartoons, competitions, prayers and daily Bible readings – dive in and get to know God and His Word.

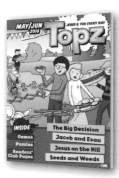

Available as an annual subscription or as single issues, published every two months.

For current prices and to order go to **www.cwr.org.uk/topzeveryday**

Or call **01252 784700** or visit a Christian bookshop.

TOPZ SPECIAL EDITIONS

TOPZ FOR NEW CHRISTIANS
Thirty days of Bible notes to help you find faith in Jesus and have fun exploring your new life with Him.

TOPZ GUIDE TO THE BIBLE
This exciting guide whizzes through the Bible – what's in it, who wrote it and loads more!

TOPZ TIPS FOR SCHOOL
Full of tips and stories to help you at school, join the Topz Gang in this brilliant guide!

TOPZ ACTIVITY BIBLE
Explore God's Word with the Topz Gang as they each retell tales from the Bible just for you!

For current prices or to purchase go to **www.cwr.org.uk/topzbooks**
Or call **01252 784700** or visit a Christian bookshop.

TOPZ GOSPELS

Join the whole Topz Gang on more fun adventures as they explore each Gospel as children living in Bible times!

TOPZ SECRET DIARIES AND STORIES

Meet each of the Topz Gang in their very own diary or story – and discover things about God and yourself along the way!

For current prices or to purchase go to **www.cwr.org.uk/topzbooks**

Or call **01252 784700** or visit a Christian bookshop.